Discovering
CHESHIRE

Joan P. Alcock

The cover shows a Victorian engraving
'Old Houses in Chester'

Shire Publications, Tring, Herts.

54707.

CONTENTS

SBN 85263117 0

INTRODUCTION

'Please would you tell me', said Alice a little timidly, 'why your cat grins like that?' 'It's a Cheshire cat,' said the Duchess, 'and most of them do.'

Lewis Carroll

Cheshire as a county covers 1,000 square miles and nearly everyone has heard of the Cheshire cat and Cheshire cheese. The cat has been immortalised in the window of Daresbury church and the cheese is still produced in its white, red and, more rarely, blue varieties. It is always thought of as being predominantly a rural county although the greater part of its population lives in the towns. The rural scene is threatened firstly by the spread of existing towns and secondly by the policy of 'overspill' which either forces a small town like Winsford to expand beyond its natural setting or deliberately creates a vast complex, as at Runcorn. Industry is also invading the rural scene and within the last ten years considerable acreage has vanished under buildings or spoil heaps.

Perhaps Cheshire has been too complacent about this, as some parts of these routes will show, but in spite of this there is still a large part of the county, which, without having the scenic grandeur of some counties, is picturesque and lovely. It is regarded as flat and certainly the Cheshire plain covers the larger part of the area, though, on closer inspection, the plain is cut by streams and broken up by small hillocks. But the eastern part of Cheshire links with the Derbyshire dales to produce wild, open country, still unspoilt and untamed. The central highlands, cutting diagonally from Bickerton to Halton, also break up the flat surface.

Cheshire towns are market centres for the urban and rural population and usually have excellent small shops. Many of these are altering their character with new central development which, unfortunately, is stamping them with a certain similarity. Closer investigation reveals their individual identity. Cheshire villages are, on the whole, still unspoilt, dominated by the church, with modern development discreetly tucked out of sight. A very pleasant afternoon can be spent meandering quietly through the lanes contrasting old and new.

Chester — Shotwick — Puddington — Burton — Neston — Parkgate — Thurstaston — West Kirby — Hoylake — Moreton — New Brighton — Birkenhead — Upton — Port Sunlight — Bromborough — Willaston — Chester (about 70 miles).

The Wirral is eighteen miles by seven and, hemmed in by the Dee and the Mersey, it gives Cheshire its characteristic shape. The northern part is classified as 'Merseyside conurbation' and is being covered by residential and industrial growth. There are still pleasant places to visit, especially on the Dee estuary, where the silting up of the river was perhaps a blessing in disguise. The route is a long one but can be done in a day.

Leave **Chester** by the Hoylake road (A540) which became the main road when it was turnpiked in 1787; before that date it ran parallel to the shore, passing through Shotwick and Puddington. Pass the outskirts of **Mollington** and take A5117 towards Queensferry. In the distance are the Shotton ironworks set against a background of the Welsh hills. Turn right (A550) at the traffic lights and, in half a mile, turn left to **Shotwick,** a tiny village, now a few houses, a hall and a church, whose cobbled street once rang with the clatter of hooves.

This was the point where the Dee was forded, for here the river once reached the church wall. The ford was in use until the nineteenth century and the sands shifted so often that the guides had to be sure that their knowledge was up-to-date. Later, two ferries made the crossing safer. Inside the porch of the fourteenth century church are long scars said to have been made by archers sharpening their arrowheads while waiting to cross. Notice the rare three-decker pulpit, the large rocks acting as weights for the clock and the box-pews. The old road from Chester to Neston runs beside the church wall; it was possibly Roman and was certainly a salt track. In the fifteenth century there is a reference to 'Saltesway, which is the Kyng's Hyghway ner Chester to lede the host of our Sovreyn Lord the Kyng in tyme of warre unto Shotwyk Ford'.

Return to the main road and turn left. At A540 turn left and go left again towards **Puddington.** Peaceful and charming, set around a green, it won the award for Cheshire's best kept village in 1969. The road to Burton swings round the hall, which was the home of the Massey family for 700 years

4

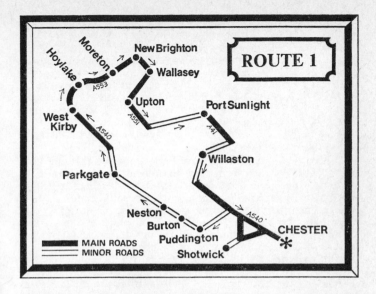

ROUTE 1

until the last member died in Chester Castle, awaiting trial
for his part in the 1715 Jacobite rebellion.

At the T-junction turn left into **Burton,** sheltered by a
wooded ridge. It once claimed to be the prettiest village in the
Wirral and there is still a quiet dignity about the houses,
many built directly on the sandstone outcrop. Burton Manor
is a residential college for adult education; a list of courses
can be obtained from the warden. Opposite the manor gates
is the thatched cottage where Thomas Wilson was born in
1663. He became Bishop of Sodor and Man and lived a 'holy,
wise and god-fearing' life from 1697 to 1755 in what was then
a very poor see. The church stands high above the village.
In the churchyard are memorials to two Catholic priests —
Ralph Platt, who died in 1827, and William Plumpton,
chaplain to the Massey family, who was executed at Chester
in 1679, a victim of the Popish Plot.

Beyond the village the road divides. Take the left fork
leading to a wide view across the estuary. The river began
to silt up in the fourteenth century and Chester lost its
prominence as a port. Sandbanks grew firmer, bound together
by the marsh grasses. Although the green carpet looks flat
it is very treacherous, hiding gullies and mud holes. Charles
Kingsley wrote his poem *Oh Mary, go and call the cattle home*

after hearing a story of a girl who was lost on the marsh when
The rolling mist came down and hid the land
And never home came she.

The road swings inland to join the direct Burton-Neston road. Turn left and just beyond is the entrance to the University of Liverpool's botanical gardens (open to visitors). Proceed to **Neston.** The church has four stained glass windows designed by Burne-Jones and made by William Morris. Emma Lyon, later Lady Hamilton, was baptised here in 1765. Turn left along B5135 to Parkgate. The road meets the estuary at a new pub—the Olde Quay.

During the eighteenth century **Parkgate** was a thriving port. John Wesley sailed from here to Ireland; so did Handel in 1741 — a new oratorio *Messiah* packed in his luggage. Stage coaches arrived from London and Liverpool. Entertainment was needed for the waiting passengers so assembly rooms were built for balls and gambling. By the end of the century it had become a fashionable spa but this could not last. Within living memory water has lapped the quay, now the marsh stretches for two miles. Go along the quay passing Mostyn Hall school (one famous pupil was Grenfell of Labrador), the Ship Inn, first built in 1571, the old assembly rooms with their ornate balcony, and the watch tower, jutting out into the road, opposite the slipway where cargoes were landed.

Follow the road inland, and turn left at the Hoylake road which passes through Heswall. Soon a view of the sea appears in the distance, for from the higher ground the end of the Wirral can be seen. **Thurstaston** is to the left where a road leads to the shore. The hall dates from 1680 but the church is relatively modern, built by Pearson, architect of Truro cathedral. Beyond the turning to Thurstaston, A540 cuts across the common bought by Birkenhead corporation in 1879 to preserve it as an open space. The red sandstone rocks thrust up through gorse and heather.

Soon, turn left along B5140 to **Caldy,** an estate village owned by the Barton family in the nineteenth century but now a hospital. Take B5141 to West Kirby and just before the Moby Dick turn down a road to the left (Sandy Lane). The pub (1964) has whaling maps and harpoons on the walls and door handles made of whales' teeth. At **West Kirby** go along the main street. Most roads on the left lead to the shore for now the Dee is merging with the sea. The mild climate of West Kirby makes it a popular residential area. At the end of the street turn right, then left, to rejoin the

Hoylake road. Grange Hill is crowned with an obelisk and there are extensive views from the top.

Follow Meols Road, pass the Royal Liverpool Golf Club and, at the roundabout, bear left along the King's Gap — so called because William III used this route in 1690 on his way to Ireland. There would be no houses then, only marshland and the open shore off which the ships anchored. When the tide is out today a large expanse of sand can be seen. Stanley Road, to the left, leads to the mouth of the estuary and there is a good view of the Hilbre Islands (see page 47). At the end of the King's Gap, follow the promenade. Half way along yachts lie at confused angles or are held lazily at anchor according to the state of the tide. When the promenade ends bear round to the right, turn right at the T-junction for Wallasey (A553), turn left at the give way sign and left again to join the main Wallasey road which rises to pass Meols station. There was once a submerged forest here, its tree trunks pressing on ferns and lichen. Collections of objects found in the peat are in Chester and Liverpool museums.

In the distance is Bidston Hill; on the top is the windmill and the white-domed observatory. At **Moreton** turn left for New Brighton at the mock Tudor Coach and Horses. Away to the left is the old Moreton lighthouse which was in use until 1908. The huge embankment protects the low-lying land for once Bidston marshes extended from the hills to the sea and were continually flooded. Leasowe Castle is on the road to New Brighton. The octagonal stone tower is part of the original castle built by Ferdinand, Earl of Derby, to guard the point of embarkation to the Stanley estates in the Isle of Man. Gradually more parts were added to it so that it assumed its ramshackle appearance. It passed through various hands until it was bought in 1910 for a railway's convalescent home.

After two miles turn left towards **New Brighton** promenade (Greenleas Road). Wallasey Golf Club is opposite the huge church of St. Nicholas — the golfers' church. The high sea wall was built as protection from the gales but its massive bulk means that for two miles there are only glimpses of the sea; ahead of us in the distance lies the varied skyline of Liverpool. New Brighton (see page 52) is a great contrast to Hoylake with an emphasis on seaside entertainment. The fort was built in 1827 to defend the Mersey and did so again in 1940 when anti-aircraft guns were placed on it. The lighthouse is now automatically controlled from the land. Opposite the pier, turn up Victoria Road and at the traffic lights turn left along Rowton Street. The route runs parallel to the Mersey and glimpses of Liverpool docks can be seen down the streets to the left. Pass **Wallasey** Town Hall and after a petrol station, turn right, along Borough Road. At the third set of traffic lights turn left down Poulton Bridge Road (B5088) towards Birkenhead docks. Cross over the bridge — a swing one to allow ships access to Wallasey Pool — and, at the end of the road, take A553 for Hoylake. (A road leads from here to Birkenhead town centre, see page 42). Turn left at the modern church of Holy Cross to ascend Bidston Hill which Birkenhead corporation have also bought to keep as an open space. The observatory specialises in predicting the height and times of the tides and tide-tables are worked out here for British ports.

At the give way sign turn right to go down the hill and go straight on at the roundabout. **Upton** has always been an important centre, for five roads met here, resulting in a weekly market. The church is modern but it contains a copy of the 'Breeches Bible' and a plaster model (original in Chester Museum) of a runic stone which translated means 'The people planted a memorial . . . . . Pray for Athelmund'.

In the centre of Upton turn left along A551 and, at the next roundabout, notice the gates of Arrowe Park with their arrow motif. Inside the park a statue of a boy scout commemorates the World Jamboree held there in 1929 — the twenty-first anniversary. Keep on A551. Thingwall was probably the meeting place of the *thing* or parliament of the Wirral Norsemen. A551 is the quickest route to Chester but to see Port Sunlight look for the Fox and Hounds on the right, then take the first left turn (Storeton Lane). After a mile Storeton Hall, famous for its Friesian herds, marks the beginning of the Lever Causeway, an avenue of trees leading to the built-up villages of **Higher and Lower Bebington.** When the causeway ends turn right, then left (Broadway) to go down to the roundabout. Turn right here; a little further is the modern church of Christchurch. In the porch is a slab showing the footprints of *Cheirotherium*, a kangaroo-like creature, which lived during the Triassic age. The prints were found in 1838 in a stratum of rock 60 feet below the ground surface.

The road eventually ends at Bebington's village green. Turn right and, beyond the Rose and Crown, pass the Meyer Free Library which houses the large collection of books left by Meyer, originally a Staffordshire man, to the people of Bebington. Bear left for **Port Sunlight** and take the first turn left (Ellens Lane) to reach the model village (described on page 50). After the visit return to the main road which continues past the railway sidings linking the private docks at Bromborough Pool with the main railway line. Keep on through **Bromborough.** The old market cross retains its original base but the shaft and carved head are Victorian. Most Cheshire crosses have had to be restored, for they lost their shafts in the seventeenth century on the orders of a puritan parliament. After Bromborough join the dual carriageway for Chester. Keep on the Chester road for two miles, then, after passing the junction with the Ellesmere Port road, turn right along B5133. **Willaston** is two miles from the turn, a quiet village set round a green. The Nag's Head dates from 1733 and the National Westminster Bank occupies a building of 1616. Turn left for Chester (B5151) passing the hall built in 1558.

In one mile the Chester — Hoylake road is reached. At the corner is the Willaston Stone, shaped like a mounting block with three steps. One suggestion is that it marked the meeting place of the hundred and thus the name Willaston is derived from Wirhael-stone. Turn left for Chester.

Route 2

Chester — Rowton — Huxley — Tarporley — Oulton Park — Little Budworth — Over — Winsford — Whitegate — Sandiway — Delamere Forest — Tarvin — Chester (40 miles).

Leave **Chester** by the Whitchurch road (A41) which is built up as far as Rowton. A road to the right crosses the Civil War battlefield. In September 1645 a Parliamentary force defeated the Royalists while Charles I watched in despair from the cathedral tower. Charles deserved this defeat. Sir Marmaduke Langdale, the Royalist commander, beat off one attack and sent Sir Geoffrey Shakerley to report to the king. Shakerley saved a ten mile detour by crossing the Dee in a tub, but Charles hesitated and all was lost. Now the heathland has been reclaimed and fields cover the site.

Go through **Rowton** and take a left turn (just past Rowton service station) for Hargrave and Huxley. Keep on along Common Lane past the new **Waverton** primary school which replaces the one provided by the Duke of Westminster for his tenants. Waverton church was restored in the nineteenth century. Above the south door is a worn statuette of the Virgin and Child placed between shields bearing arms of the

9

Dutton and Hatton families. Presently a tall bank on the left hides the Shropshire Union Canal, dug in 1776 and in constant use until this century for bringing goods to Waverton, thus by-passing the bad roads. Cross the canal, take the right fork and a little further bear left for Huxley. The range of hills in the distance has Bickerton Hill at its southern end and isolated Beeston Crag at the northern.

Huxley is a scattered village. In the last century the Cheshire historian, Ormerod, wrote that this part was flat and uninteresting but it has a pleasant rural character, highlighted by the distant hills. Turn right opposite the gate of Elm Tree Farm and follow the signs for Tarporley entering by A49. **Tarporley** lies on the main Chester-London road which was so important that it was turnpiked as early as 1742. The Rising Sun and the Swan are old hostelries and the main street has many pleasant buildings. St. Helen's church contains memorials of the Crewe family: Sir John wrings his hands to Heaven and Mary surveys her world from the table-top tomb. In the Civil War Sir William Brereton met the Royalists at Rhuddall Heath; some of their armour was placed in the church.

Turn right along A49 towards Warrington. At the top of the rise turn right for Eaton and immediately go left down the hill. At the main road in Eaton go left towards Northwich, then take the second turn on the right (Beech Lane) for **Oulton.** Pass the mill built in 1781, which looks across the lake, and cross Budworth Common, covered with birch trees and pleasant walking country. The entrance to Oulton Park racing circuit is on the right. Only the gateway remains of the estate which Sir John Vanbrugh designed for Sir Philip Egerton in 1716, for the house was burned in 1926 and was bombed in 1940. At **Little Budworth** swing round the church in which the Egertons and their servants are buried.

Pass Budworth Pool, turn right at the give way sign and then go right again towards Winsford. At **Over** St. Chad's is now the parish church of Winsford. Legend says that it was built elsewhere and the Devil removed it but as he was flying overhead the monks of Vale Royal began to 'rongen' their bells. In alarm he dropped the church which gently descended to its present spot. Over is traditionally the birthplace of Robert Nixon, the Cheshire prophet.

At **Winsford** (see page 52) go down the hilly main street and, just before the bridge over the river Weaver, turn left towards Vale Royal. The valley is disfigured by salt working which intensified here in the nineteenth century. The route passes Britain's last working rock salt mine but it was the

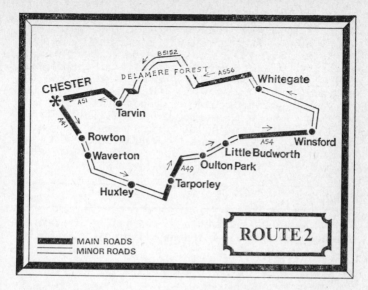

ROUTE 2

pumping of brine in the last century which caused subsidence elsewhere in Winsford to form Winsford Flashes.

Turn right at the give way sign. **Whitegate,** which also claims to be the birthplace of Nixon, lies round the triangular green on which the maypole stands. The name comes from the white gates of Vale Royal Abbey. Edward I, caught in a storm at sea in 1277, vowed that he would found a Cistercian monastery. At his request some monks came from Dore Abbey (Herefordshire) to Cheshire, settling first at Darnhall, then at Vale Royal. The king laid the foundation stone but the Black Death prevented the completion of the building. At the Dissolution in 1539 only fifteen monks remained. Sir Thomas Holcroft built himself a house from the stones thus fulfilling Nixon's prophecy that the house would become a raven's nest, for Sir Thomas' crest was a raven. Lady Cholmondeley bought it and entertained James I when he visited Cheshire in 1617. Now the house is a country club and of the great abbey nothing remains but a traced outline (revealed by excavation) and a stone to mark where the high altar stood.

To the right the view extends over parkland, once the abbey estates. A slip road to the left (signposted Chester) leads to A556. Soon **Sandiway** is reached. The Blue Cap is called after a foxhound, famous in the eighteenth century for

11

winning all its races even with a weight tied round its neck. Continue for Chester, crossing A49. Oakmere Hall to the right is now a rehabilitation centre. Turn right at Vale Royal Abbey Arms along B5152 for Frodsham. Take the first turn to the left if wishing to see the Iron Age fortress of **Eddisbury Hill** re-used in Saxon times by Edda of Mercia. If not, pass Delamere station and turn left at the Forest Cafe to run through the forest. Continue as signposted for Tarvin until the main Chester road is reached (A54). Turn right. **Tarvin** is off the main road to the left, built on a sandstone outcrop. The church bears the marks of cannonballs fired by Sir William Brereton's troops to oust the Royalists from the tower. A54 leads directly to Chester.

Route 3

Chester — Stoak — Helsby — Frodsham — Runcorn — Halton — Daresbury — Delamere Forest — Chester (40 miles).

Leave **Chester** towards Warrington. At the ring road turn left along A41 and, after a mile, turn right for Chester Zoo. This was started privately in 1930 at Oakfield House, but later the North of England Zoological Society bought it with the object of keeping animals in their natural surroundings. Beyond the entrance take the road for **Stoak.** After crossing the humpbacked bridge over the Shropshire Union Canal take the right fork and at the give way sign turn left as for Stanney. By the Bunbury Arms a right turn leads to Stoak church. This was rebuilt in 1827 but, though of little interest architecturally, it contains fourteen memorial panels showing coats of arms of the Bunbury family — a rare collection, for most such panels have been destroyed.

Beyond the Bunbury Arms the Stanlow refineries can be seen dominating the fields. The area has always been low-lying and marshy. A Cistercian abbey was founded on the banks of the Mersey in 1184 and the monks endured the constant floods until they transferred to Whalley. Today the oil refinery spreads across the once monastic land. Turn right at the main road, A5117. **Helsby Hill,** an abrupt scarp of Keuper sandstone owned by the National Trust, rises in the distance, giving a wide view from the Celtic fort on the summit. The quarries below provided stone for the building of Chester and Liverpool cathedrals and Birkenhead docks.

A5117 joins A56, a busy road since Roman times for it

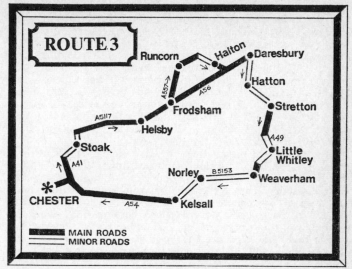

ROUTE 3

MAIN ROADS
MINOR ROADS

was the only route between the marsh and the hills. The castle at Frodsham guarded the passage until it was destroyed in the Civil War. **Frodsham,** unusually for Cheshire, has a wide main street which allowed stage coaches to draw on to the cobbles. The Bear's Paw and the Queen's Head are old hostelries. St. Lawrence's has good church furnishings and some curious epitaphs. Continue along A56 crossing the Weaver and the Weaver Navigation Canal. Occasionally there is a wait when the bridge opens to allow a ship to pass. In 1721 a scheme was devised to make the Weaver navigable and within two years boats carrying tons of rock salt went from Northwich to Frodsham.

Turn left, just beyond the bridge, for **Runcorn** along A557. (Alternatively go on and join the route again at Daresbury.) The North Cheshire motorway will cut across this part and signs of its progress are already evident. Follow the signs for town centre. On leaving Runcorn take A533 for Northwich, then A558 for Warrington. A road branches off for Halton, formerly a country lane, now passing through housing estates, for Runcorn is being developed to provide for a population of 90,000 (see also page 50). **Halton,** perched on the hill, once seemed a Gothic creation topped by a church spire; now it stands in a sea of houses. At Halton turn along Church Lane. From the square outside the castle there is a superb view stretching westward to the Runcorn bridges. Helsby lies to the south, Norton water tower sails on top of the crest to the east. It was one of the finest views in the county for its effect of space and light. What will remain in the future? The castle was built by Robert Nigel, 1st Baron Halton, soon after 1066. It became part of the Duchy of Lancaster and is still its property. In the sixteenth century it was a prison and, needless to say, was garrisoned in the Civil War, but ruined in 1644. The church is mainly Victorian, the rectory Georgian and nearby is Sir John Chessyre's library, endowed in 1733 and, apart from Chetham's at Manchester, the oldest public library in the north.

Return to the main street to leave along the Northwich road (A533). On reaching A56 turn left. When the road becomes a dual carriageway, pull over to the right to turn for **Daresbury.** Turn for Hatton opposite the old school house but stop at the church to see an unusual window dedicated to Lewis Carroll. He was baptised here in 1832 when his father was the vicar and in 1932 a memorial window was subscribed. The Cheshire Cat grins at us; the White Rabbit, the Duchess and all the other well-known characters are depicted in glass. Alice stands by Lewis Carroll (the Revd Charles Dodgson) who kneels in hood and surplice.

Continue for **Hatton** and turn right at the Hatton Arms, meeting place of the Cheshire Forest hounds. After a mile turn right at **Stretton** along A49 towards Tarporley. In three miles **Little Whitley** is by-passed. Here are the Chetwode Arms, another meeting place of the hunt, and an early seventeenth century church, with a fine nave roof. Cross the Weaver and at **Weaverham,** whose old houses grew up round a spring believed to have healing powers, turn right towards Frodsham (B5153).

Acton Bridge is a farming community, which once boasted a saltpetre factory. Bear left over the railway and in one mile turn left towards Norley and Hatchmere. **Norley** was the northern limit of Delamere and was reputed to shelter robbers who attacked travellers in the forest. Follow the signs for Hatchmere and at the crossroads by the Forest Cafe, turn right. **Hatchmere** is 100 yards along the road (plate 9), a beauty spot, reed-fringed and once the home of pike. Return to the crossroads and turn right, plunging into Delamere, splendid on an autumn day. At the next crossroads, turn left towards Kelsall and run by the side of bracken-fringed Spy Hill. **Kelsall** is in the central uplands and used to organise protection for travellers going through the forest. At Kelsall, turn right (A54) to reach Chester.

14

Route 4

Nantwich — Wybunbury — Audlem — Norbury — Malpas — Peckforton Hills — Burwardsley — Beeston Castle — Bunbury — Acton — Nantwich (55 miles).

Leave **Nantwich** (described on page 49) on A51 towards Stone and, in one mile, turn left for **Wybunbury** joining B5071 just before the village. The 94 foot high church tower dominates the village; in it, in 1969 the Rector discovered a chest containing the church plate, thought to be lost. At the end of the village, fork right and, a little further, cross A51; continue as signposted along B5071. Go through **Hatherton** and on joining A529 turn left towards Whitchurch. One mile on, cross **Hankelow's** scrubby green and soon **Audlem** is reached. Turn right at the church (A525) and, at the end of the street, keep right after crossing the canal.

For the next few miles we see some of Cheshire's finest farming country; many of the farms produce Cheshire's characteristic cheese. The land is more open than in the northern part of the county and the farms are larger. The area suffered in the 1967-68 attack of foot and mouth disease

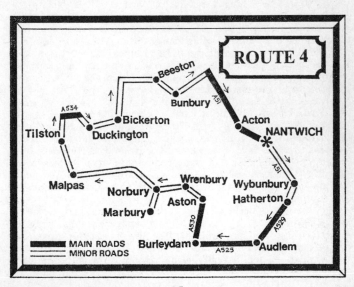

but has since been re-stocked. After **Burleydam** bear right along A5015 then turn right along A530. The gates opposite belong to Combermere Abbey, founded by Malbank, baron of Nantwich, in the twelfth century. Situated on the route from Chester to Shrewsbury, it had to provide hospitality for travellers until its dissolution in 1538.

After two miles, at **Aston,** turn left at the crossroads towards Wrenbury. Pass Aston Mill and a half-timbered house dated 1667. Keep on as signposted for Wrenbury and after bending sharply to the right pass Wrenbury station, an example of the country cottage type, now fast disappearing. Beyond the station turn left as for Tarporley. **Wrenbury** is set round a green with the church to one side. The oak pew by the porch was provided for the whipper who kept the dogs out. Bear right, signposted Bickley. After passing the Cotton Arms, an old farmhouse, cross the bridge, almost Dutch in appearance and turn left for **Norbury.** The mill is still in use; the monks of Combermere built a mill here and made their tenants grind their corn at it. Often boats are moored at the wharf on the Shropshire Union Canal. A detour can be made to **Marbury,** said to be one of the prettiest villages in south Cheshire. Though the hall has been pulled down, the view from the churchyard, looking down on to Big Mere is truly English.

Continue as signposted to Malpas. After a mile turn right for **Bickley,** then cross A49. The land is very flat; the hilly country to the south lies in Shropshire. After crossing A41 the road starts to undulate as it reaches the northern spur of the hills. When **Malpas** (see page 48) is reached turn left at the no entry sign, then right, to reach the town centre. Go through the main street and leave on the Tilston road which skirts Overton Scar. The Welsh hills lie in the distance, while Bickerton Hill stands out to the right. In the centre of **Tilston,** at the Carden Arms, turn right towards Duckington. Pass half-timbered Lower Carden Hall and a little further when the road faces the gates of Carden Hall turn right, to wind past Cliff Bank, a sandstone mass of the Peckforton group. Turn right at A534 and go straight on at the roundabout. The route can be broken here to return to Nantwich (nine miles).

To see the Cheshire hill country take the first right for **Duckington.** Pass the sign of the badger at the gates of Broxton Hall and one mile further turn left at the crossroads to go round Bickerton Hill, crowned by the Iron Age fort of Maiden Castle. At **Bickerton** church turn left and soon cross A534 to make for Harthill. On the right is Bulkeley Hill with its curious sandstone peaks. At the next junction bear right, pass Harthill church (1609) and go down the hill where the view opens out across the plain. The Peckforton Hills, rising to 746 feet, form the watershed between the Dee and the Mersey. Turn right for **Burwardsley** which nestles against the slope and a right, then a left turn brings us to the church. The nave was built in 1730, the chancel a hundred years later. Beeston Castle, perched on the top of the crag, is visible from the churchyard; the beacon signalled from there to Helsby and to Alderley Edge in times of danger.

By turning right to go up the hill a more extensive view is obtained; at the top a bridle path leads to Peckforton. By turning left we continue our journey. At the next junction turn right towards Tettenhall and one mile further turn right towards **Beeston** (see page 41). Antony Salvin built a replica of a medieval castle on the top of Peckforton Hill for Lord Tollemache about 1850. The true medieval castle is on top of Beeston Crag. When the Crag is reached either road may be taken round it. On leaving it, turn for Peckforton. After Peckforton Castle gates turn left for Bunbury along Peckforton Hall Lane. Go through Spurstow, cross A49 and turn left at the Crewe Arms. At **Bunbury** village keep to the upper road which leads to the church. Within it lies the effigy of Sir Hugh Calverley, with accurately carved plate armour. His nose has gone, ground to powder, so it is said, as a remedy for the King's Evil. Sir George Beeston's tomb recalls that he was knighted at the age of 89 for helping to fight the Spanish Armada. The reredos and the rood screen are evidence of modern craftsmanship, both carved by Fred Crossley, a Cheshire writer and woodcarver.

Beyond the church the road passes Bunbury locks which stretch back beyond Beeston to raise the canal over the Beeston foothills. At A51 turn right for Nantwich. **Acton** church is mid-fourteenth century and the interior contains the seventeenth century tomb of Sir Thomas Wilbraham; notice the wedding ring on his wife's thumb. Dorfold Hall is on the right on entering Nantwich (open once a week in summer). Built in 1616 it suffered from both Parliamentarians and Royalists in the Civil War but managed to survive. Welsh Row leads to the town centre.

Altrincham — Pickmere — Middlewich — Bostock Green
— Northwich — Great Budworth — Lymm — Rushgreen
— Warburton — Altrincham (40 miles).

From **Altrincham** (see page 41) take A56 for Northwich
following the line of Watling Street, which linked the Roman
garrison at Chester to the fort of Mancunium. Join A556
before Mere and cross the motorway. A road to the right
(B5391) leads to **Pickmere,** one of the few Cheshire meres
open to the public. The meres were formed in several ways.
Sometimes water filled the hollows left behind when the ice,
which covered the area in glacial times, had melted. At
other times deposits of rock salt in the sandstone were
dissolved leaving a space in which water could collect. The
meres have become a refuge for wild life although
occasionally, as at Budworth, they are used for sailing.
Continue along A556. The Smoker Inn dates from
Elizabethan times but the name comes from a favourite horse
of Lord de Tabley, which he often rode at reviews of the
Cheshire Yeomanry, a regiment raised by him during the
Napoleonic Wars. Soon the smoke of Northwich appears on
the horizon. Turn left along A530 for Middlewich. This is
King Street, which runs straight for four miles, part of the
Roman road coming southwards from the glass depot at
Wildespool. Finds of Roman material have been discovered
near to Middlewich where there was probably a Roman
station to exploit the salt.
Turn right at the end of King Street towards the centre
of **Middlewich** (see page 49). Take A54 for Winsford and,
after a mile, bear right for Northwich. Pass Bostock Hall,
once owned by the France Hayhurst family, now a residential
school for retarded children. The family built the estate
houses of **Bostock Green,** a village which claims to be the
centre of Cheshire. Keep on through Davenham for **Northwich**
and, after crossing the iron bridge over the Dane, go straight
on along the one-way street to the town centre (see page 49).
Take a road to the left (B5075) for Warrington, which drops
towards the salt flashes. These are due to subsidence caused
by pumping out the brine from beneath the surface. Some
are used to dump chemical refuse; others have become dry,
white flats. Yet others are the haunts of swans, ducks, coots
and anglers. The chemical works at Winnington stand out on
the skyline to the left.

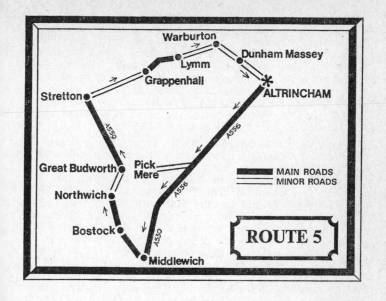

ROUTE 5

At the give way sign turn left. **Great Budworth** church rears up on the ridge dominating the houses clustering for shelter round it. The next turn to the right leads to this charming village with its thatched cottages, jutting porches and wayside gardens. The picturesque George Inn lies opposite the church which has a magnificent sixteenth century nave roof. Return to the cross roads and turn right (A559) for Warrington passing the Cock O'Budworth, an eighteenth century coaching inn and present meeting place of the Cheshire Forest hounds. A559 meets B5356 at **Stretton** church; turn right for Lymm.

Go through **Appleton** and, just beyond the disused military camp, keep straight on down Broad Lane to **Grappenhall** noting the view across the Mersey valley and the haze of Warrington in the distance. Keep to the main road and, after crossing the Bridgewater Canal, turn right. At the traffic lights keep on as signposted to Lymm and Altrincham. Ahead rises the huge, satisfying curve of the bridge which carries the M6 over the Mersey and over the Manchester Ship Canal, rising high enough to let the ships pass underneath.

Turn left along B5158 to Partington and Warrington,

descending to **Lymm** village, which lies round a pond overflowing into a deep gully. The village cross, in the cobbled square, was restored for the Diamond Jubilee of Queen Victoria. The lower steps are hewn from solid rock and at their foot is a replica of the village stocks. At the top of the street is the Bridgewater Canal dug by James Brindley for the Duke. The latter was determined that there should be no locks so that the canal could be as level as possible but this meant, as at Lymm, that often the banks were raised above the level of the surrounding country.

Cross the canal and go through the straggling houses of **Rushgreen,** its name a memory of the time when rushes were gathered to cover the church floor. The custom was revived in 1970. After crossing the railway and the river, turn left for Hollings Green (B5159). **Warburton** is reached in half a mile. The village still has the base and steps of the market cross and the stocks, whose left post has hand clasps for a whipping post. From the green a road leads to the old church, dedicated to St. Werburgh, patron saint also of Chester cathedral, and dating from 1190. The north wall still shows timber framing packed with wattle and daub, last restored in 1958. Outside is a tall yew tree, said to be contemporary with the building of the first church. The village was founded over a thousand years ago by Queen Aethelfleda of Mercia as one of a chain of forts which kept back invaders from the north.

A road leads to the toll bridge which originally bridged the Mersey but due to change of course is over a dry river bed. Tolls are still charged but it is worth paying to mount the ramp and look back on the view from the Manchester Ship Canal bridge.

Take Paddock Lane to return to the main road. Warburton new church, a Victorian one, rears up to the right. At the main road turn left and pass the Saracens Head whose name recalls an incident in the crusades when Lord de Warburton decapitated a Saracen chieftain. Take the next turn right (at Warburton post office) towards Altrincham. Continue for **Dunham Massey.** Go over the railway line towards Dunham Town and just beyond follow the sign for Dunham Woodhouses, so called because the estate woodmen lived there. Soon the road runs along the wall of Dunham Hall. The estate was held by Lord Delamere but eventually passed to the Earls of Stamford who open the grounds to the public. Take B5160 still following the wall and, half a mile further, turn left along A56 for Altrincham.

Route 6

Altrincham — Ashley — Mobberley — Wilmslow — Alderley Edge — Capesthorne Hall — Siddington — Jodrell Bank — Over Peover — Lower Peover — Knutsford — Tatton Park — Rostherne — Altrincham (about 45 miles).

Take A538 from **Altrincham** and, at the traffic lights along Ashley Road, turn left for Hale (B5163). About a mile further proceed for Ashley and after crossing the railway follow the signpost for Knutsford. Signposts will then direct for Mobberley. At **Ashley** coal and other goods were unloaded for the Tatton estate; sometimes deer arrived to restock the park. The Greyhound Inn was originally a farmhouse; the sign, a repainting of the original, depicts one of the favourite dogs of Lord Egerton of Tatton.

At Ashley crossroads go straight on and proceed to **Mobberley** church, which has been associated with the Leigh Mallory family for centuries. In one aisle is a most unusual window, possibly the only one in the country to depict Everest in stained glass. George Leigh Mallory and his companion,

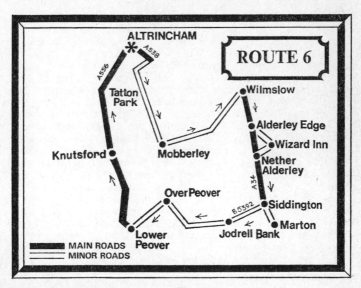

21

Andrew Irving, disappeared into the mist while making a final attempt on the summit of the mountain in 1924. Twenty years later his brother, Air Chief Marshall Sir Trafford Leigh Mallory, was killed with his wife in a plane crash in the Alps and a memorial plaque to them was placed beneath this window. The church itself is small, dating from 1254, but the upper part and the nave roof supported by angels date from 1450. The organ was given by Sir Charles Hallé, founder of the orchestra, and once stood in the Free Trade Hall, Manchester. In the churchyard is a yew tree with a spread of sixty feet and in its shade, on the outer side of the wall, are the village stocks.

Pass the church and, at B5085, turn left to wind through the village with its scattered houses. Behind the high yew hedge on the left is the old hall, red brick with mullioned windows. Follow the signs for Wilmslow. The next village is **Lindow** or **Row-of-Trees,** marked by a row of lime trees, planted in the seventeenth century. In the distance appears the sandstone ridge of Alderley Edge. Fork left along B5086, a road lined with pleasant houses which leads to the roundabout on the outskirts of **Wilmslow.** Bear left if wishing to visit the town (described on page 52), if not take A34 for **Alderley Edge** (see page 41).

At the end of Alderley main street take a road on the left leading to the Edge which winds up the hill between large houses. The Wizard Inn recalls the legend of the wizard who showed the farmer the armed men asleep under the Edge and the gold stored within it. Turn right at the inn to descend into **Nether Alderley** down Artists Lane, a tree-lined route with views over the plain. The cottages along the lane were the homes of the miners and others are grouped round the preaching cross where the lane joins A34. Turn left for Congleton. Soon after, notice the sixteenth century mill with its long sloping roof. It was in use until 1939 and, owned by the National Trust, it is gradually being restored. A road on the right leads to the seventeenth century school standing by the gate of the church. The latter has a huge pew straddling the south aisle, used by the Stanleys, lords of the manor from 1560 to 1938. Edward Stanley, later Bishop of Norwich, was vicar here for thirty years and wrote a minor classic *The Familiar History of Birds*. His son, Arthur, author of the *Life of Dr. Arnold* and Dean of Westminster, was born here in 1815. The Stanley home was at Alderley Park, further along A34, now owned by I.C.I. Go straight on at Monks Heath crossroads (traffic lights) so called because monks from Combermere Abbey settled here.

Capesthorne Hall (open to the public) has been owned by the Bromley-Davenport family since 1722 but most of the hall dates from after a fire in 1861. Anthony Salvin, architect of Peckforton Castle, did the rebuilding in the Jacobean style. To the left is Redesmere, famous for its bird life and for its legend of the floating island. Once a year Fanshawe fete is held with the local children playing the parts of the lady of the lake and the knight-cavalier. A road to the left (signposted Henbury) leads to the lake.

At the next crossroads notice **Siddington** church on the left. Only the porch and chancel are timber framed, the rest was replaced by painted stone in the eighteenth century. Our route turns right here but nearly two miles further along A34 at **Marton** is a most unusual medieval church perched above the main road. The timbers slope from the ridge beam to the outer walls and it seems as if it would be more at home in Scandinavia.

Turn right at Siddington along B5392 and just beyond, keep left. We have left a turnpike road for one of the oldest in the county, a cross-country packhorse trail along which salt was sent from Middlewich through the Derbyshire hills to the eastern counties. One of the farms is called Salterslane, which recalls the old use. The next village is **Lower Withington.** Keep to the right of the triangular green, passing the Methodist chapel built in 1808. At the end bear right and a quarter of a mile further keep left. The radio telescope looms above the trees. Turn right along A535 and in one mile turn left towards **Jodrell Bank.** The huge bowl, completed in 1957, has been joined by a smaller one and the work of the telescope is explained in the concourse buildings which are open to the public. After Jodrell go over the railway and bear right. At the end of the narrow lane turn right, cross Peover Eye — the glittering stream — and at the end of this lane turn left towards Knutsford. Half a mile further, bear left at **Over Peover** post office.

A footpath leads from here to Over Peover Hall and church, which were in the possession of the Mainwaring family for 500 years. Sir Roger built the Elizabethan hall and his wife added the Stuart stables decorated with carved woodwork and plaster ceilings. (The latter have recently been opened to the public). During 1944 the hall was the headquarters of General Patton, commander of the American Third Army, who presented an American flag which still hangs in the church. The church was the family chapel; it was rebuilt in the nineteenth century but the Mainwaring monuments remain.

23

Continue until A50 is reached, then turn left. This was the main road from London to the North until the M6 was built. The Whipping Stocks inn has served travellers since the sixteenth century and the former toll house is by its side. Go south along A50 for two miles, then turn right at the crossroads towards Northwich along Townfield Lane. At the T-junction turn right; **Lower Peover** is reached in half a mile. A wooden signpost on the right indicates a cobbled lane leading to the Bells O'Peover, the church and the school — essential ingredients of village life. The church is akin to the one at Marton but in 1853 the roof, which covered the whole church, was altered to make separate roofs over the nave and aisles. Inside are box-pews, with family crests on the doors, stout wooden pillars supporting dark roof beams, and a large chest with a heavy lid, which a woman had to lift with one hand before she was considered fit to be a farmer's wife. In the churchyard a huge Celtic cross marks the grave of Lord de Tabley, a neglected Cheshire poet. The family name was given to the Bells O'Pcover but few people would recognise this old inn, which once housed the priest, as the Warren de Tabley Arms. The old schoolhouse, built in 1710, is still used as an annexe of the newer one.

Return along the lane and turn right. Go along B5081 and at A50 turn left for Knutsford. Soon **Toft** church is on the right and Toft Hall on the left. The former was built in 1854, the latter, approached by an avenue of elms, was the home of the Leycester family but during the Second World War it became a prisoner of war camp. The name Toft may indicate that Norsemen settled here in the tenth century.

Pass **Knutsford** court house, built with the profits from the Weaver Navigation Canal, and leave by A50 (the town is described on page 48). Over two miles further turn right along A5034 for **Tatton Park.** Take the second road to the right, which runs along the estate wall, before reaching the main gates. This was the home of the Egertons from 1598 until it was handed over to the National Trust on the death of the last Lord Egerton. The house was rebuilt in 1780 to the designs of Samuel Wyatt, who incorporated the eighteenth century dining room and added the huge south portico, composed of four columns, each twenty feet high, and each carved from one block of Runcorn stone. Other attractions, especially in the spring, are the rhododendrons and azaleas and a Japanese garden.

Opposite the gates a road runs to **Rostherne,** huddled in a dip by the mere. The churchyard is entered by a gate, made in the seventeenth century but a forerunner of the automatic

24

George H. Haines

1. *The two Saxon crosses at Sandbach (Route 7) are thought to have been erected by Peada, son of Penda of Mercia, to mark his conversion to Christianity.*

George H. Haines

2. *The strange cross by the school in Delamere Street, Wins-ford (Route 2) has a lock-up beneath its base, accessible from behind the steps.*

British Waterways Board

3. *The Anderton Lift near Northwich (Route 5) was opened in 1875 to lift barges from the Trent and Mersey canal to the river Weaver.*

George H. Haines

4. *From King Charles' Tower on the east wall of Chester, Charles I is said to have watched his troops defeated at the battle of Rowton Moor. An exhibition is on display here, with relics of the Civil War.*

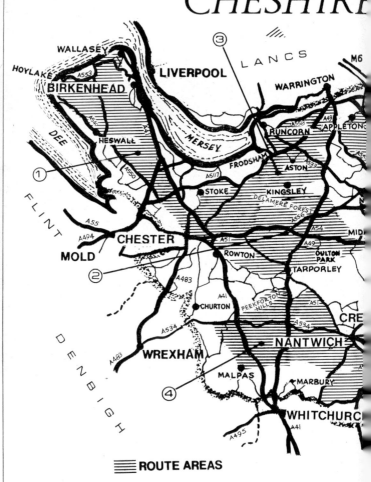

CHESHIRE

ROUTE AREAS

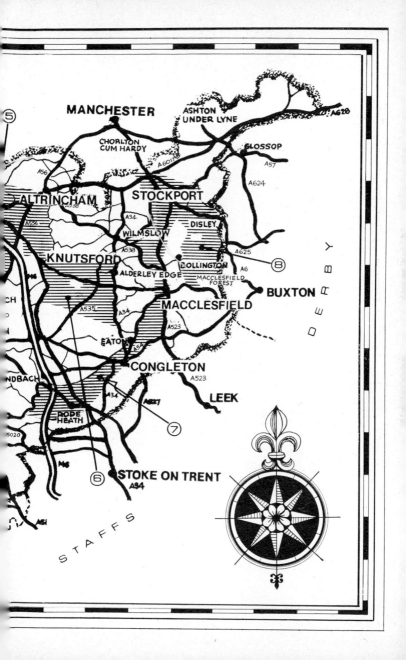

5. *One of the many fine carvings in Chester Cathedral.*

George H. Haines

6. *The view of Rostherne Mere (Route 6) from the church. The mere is a nature reserve and contains a variety of fish.*

7. *Little Moreton Hall (Route 7) is one of Cheshire's finest black and white buildings. It is open to the public.*

George H. Haines

E. Preston

8. *The curtain walls of Beeston Castle (Route 4), built in 1225 by the Earl of Chester and later captured from the Parliamentarians during the Civil War by a party of only nine Royalists.*

9. *Hatchmere Lake in Delamere Forest (Route 3) is a favourite beauty spot.*

E. Preston

ones. The church contains the effigy of Sir Hugh Venables carved about 1250; notice how lightly he grips his sword and how his mail gauntlets are thrown back at the wrists to leave his hands bare. The Egertons of Tatton are buried here. One memorial, by Westmacott, is to the pathetic Charlotte Egerton drowned in the mere on her wedding eve. Rostherne mere, and 400 acres round it, became a nature reserve in 1961 and to preserve its biological importance access is limited to naturalists. It contains a variety of fish including smelt, a sea water fish, but here, most unusually, found in fresh water (plate 6).

Continue past the church; the mere can be seen at intervals on the right. Turn right for Altrincham along A556. **Bowden** church rears on the ridge ahead of us. After just a mile take A56 for **Altrincham.**

Route 7

Stockport — Adlington Hall — Macclesfield — Bosley — Cloud — Astbury — Little Moreton Hall — Barthomley — Sandbach — Congleton — Gawsworth — Prestbury — Stockport (70 miles).

From **Stockport** (see page 51) leave by the A6 and at Hazel Grove take A523 for Macclesfield which soon gives a view of the plain and the hills. Pass **Poynton** on to the Legh Arms where a turn on the right leads to Adlington Hall, owned by the Legh family since 1315. The mixture of styles, inside and out, provides contrast and charm. The great hall, begun in 1486, has an eighteenth century organ on which Handel is reputed to have played and a hammerbeam roof decorated with coats of arms of Cheshire families. Sir Thomas Legh, High Sheriff of Cheshire at the time of the Armada, added the half-timbered wing; in the 1740s Charles Legh built the Georgian wing and the stables.

Continue along A523 through **Tytherington** and, on entering **Macclesfield** (see page 48), turn left as signposted A523 for Leek. Three huge housing blocks, the first in this part of Cheshire, rear up at the front but the hills rise higher behind. Follow the signs for Leek and turn left at the traffic lights. In one mile the huge Moss Rose public house is in turn dominated by the newly built stand of Macclesfield Football Club, founded in 1889. Further on a toll house shows the characteristic bow-fronted window from which the keeper kept watch for travellers.

The hills begin to press on the road on one side and running parallel on the other is the Macclesfield Canal, opened in 1831 to carry goods between the Trent and Mersey and the Peak Forest canals. Fool's Nook, in spite of its unusual inn sign, is probably fowl's nook, a place where wild fowls rested. Go over the crossroads and through the scattered village of **Bosley,** passing the Harrington Arms, where once a year the tenants paid rent to the Earl of Harrington. Bosley Cloud is seen on the right. At the bottom of the descent turn right along the road (signposted Tunstall and Biddulph) which leads to Dane Wood Mill, once a cotton mill, now used for grinding sawdust into wood flour. The road bends sharply at the narrow bridge over the Dane and then winds its way upwards to emerge on a ledge overlooking the plain.

The Cloud, rising to 1190 feet, with a view from the top extending eastward to the Peak District and westward across Cheshire, was once part of the Egerton estate but is now owned by the National Trust. Far in the distance are the Peckforton Hills and the isolated hill crowned by **Beeston** Castle; the huge white bowl is the Jodrell Bank telescope. Just below, to the right, is the viaduct which carried the old North Staffordshire Railway across the Dane Valley. The effects of the light across the plain seem reminiscent of Dutch painting, nothing startling, but soothing and cool.

The road drops to the small settlement of **Timbersbrook.** Follow the road round to the right, go over the crossroads (keep the cafe on the left) and climb up the shoulder of the next ridge where another wide view appears. At the Coach and Horses with its spirited inn sign bear right down the hill. Cross the Congleton-Biddulph road (A527), go along Leek Road (a turnpike road of 1795) and turn left along Moss Road leading to Astbury. The ridge on the left is Congleton Edge which forms the watershed between the Mersey and the Trent. Cross the railway and the Macclesfield Canal. In the distance is the spire of **Astbury** church, one of the largest in Cheshire. The village green is covered with daffodils in the spring. The churchyard contains an unusual canopied tomb and from here the sweep of the village is visible — the inn, modern village hall, Georgian rectory, Victorian school. The church is mainly Perpendicular, with eighteenth century box-pews and a medieval rood screen. There are two fine tombs — Sir John Davenport in thirteenth century armour and Lady Egerton in stiff Tudor dress.

At the bottom of the green turn left along A34. **Little Moreton Hall** soon comes into view. One of Cheshire's finest black and white buildings, it was built in the sixteenth century

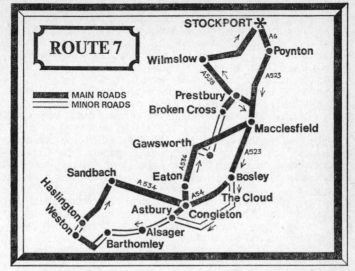

ROUTE 7

MAIN ROADS
MINOR ROADS

STOCKPORT
Poynton
A6
Wilmslow
A523
A538
Prestbury
Broken Cross
Macclesfield
Gawsworth
A523
A556
Sandbach
Eaton
Bosley
A534
A54
The Cloud
Astbury
Congleton
Haslington
Weston
Alsager
Barthomley

as a farmhouse. It is owned by the National Trust and is open to visitors. The view of the house from across the moat with its overhanging porch, carved gables and multipaned windows is outstanding (plate 7).

Continue along A34. The hills on the left are crowned by Mow Cop Castle, a folly built about 1750 by Randle Wilbraham to mark the boundary of his estate. Below the castle was the first camp site of the Primitive Methodists. Just over a mile from Moreton Hall turn right down Church Lane towards Rode Heath. Beyond Odd Rode church the road bends left round Rode Pool. At the crossroads turn left along A50 and a little further at the Lawton Arms turn right (B5077) to **Alsager** which is expanding rapidly as it becomes a commuter town for the Potteries.

Leaving the outskirts of Alsager turn left down the road marked R.O.F. Radway Green, pass the munitions factory and rise to pass over the motorway. At this point one can see how much agricultural land Cheshire had to sacrifice to motoring needs. Soon **Barthomley** is reached. During the Second World War a company of the South Staffordshire Regiment was stationed here. Their stay was peaceful but in the Civil War a visit by Royalist cavalry had a grim sequal for they drove the villagers into the church and slaughtered many of them.

Turn right at the church and left at the next junction (signposted Weston). One mile further bear left again. Here is the small village of **Englesea Brook,** a centre of Primitive Methodism. The chapel was built in 1826 and the tiny cemetery contains the remains of a dozen families, staunch followers of Hugh Bourne. He also lies here under the inscribed monument at the end of the path.

Turn right at the next crossroads and go right again at A52. On either side stretches a wide open view. During spring the rich ploughland stands out in the chequer board of green fields. The soil includes clays and glacial sands which give the earth its reddish colour. By following A52 Nantwich can be reached, but bear right along A5020 signposted for Crewe. After **Weston,** take a right fork (signposted Alsager). Crewe Hall stands out between the trees to the right, built in 1866 to replace a Jacobean house burnt down in that year. While the house burned Lord Crewe is said to have telegraphed to the architect, Sir Charles Barry, 'Crewe is burning. Come and build it up again'. He did and imitated the parapets and central tower of the old house.

At the next junction turn towards Crewe and after almost a mile, do not follow the main road bearing left but cut across it and go straight on. At the next junction Crewe is to the left but our route turns right along A534 through **Haslington** for Sandbach. Pass Winterley Pool and at **Sandbach** (page 51) keep on A534. The motorway is crossed and just beyond is another fine half-timbered house. In the distance on the right is Sandbach Heath with its Victorian Gothic church. **Arclid** crossroads are controlled by traffic lights and the large building behind the inn, now a hospital, was the old union workhouse. The Pennines become a backcloth to **Congleton** and when that town is reached (page 46) take A536 for Macclesfield.

Go through **Eaton,** a centre of Quaker activity in the seventeenth century, and four miles beyond is **Gawsworth.** Turn right at the crossroads here by the post office along a road leading past the village cross to New Hall, now an old peoples' home. It was built in 1712 for Lord Mohun but he never occupied it for in that year he fought a duel with the Duke of Hamilton and each killed the other. The Old Hall, half timbered and in an equally lovely setting, is open to visitors. An avenue of limes, planted in 1827, leads from the church to the Harrington Arms, a Queen Anne hostelry. The Fittons were the lords of the manor until the sixteenth century; some of their elaborate memorials are in the church. Mary Fitton is reputed to have been Shakespeare's 'Dark Lady of the

Sonnets' and was depicted as such by the Cheshire novelist, Beatrice Tunstall. The view from the church, looking across the pool to New Hall, is one of the loveliest in Cheshire.

Return to the crossroads. For a direct route to Stockport turn right for Macclesfield. Opposite the Rising Sun is Dane's Moss where peat is still cut. Beyond are the Buxton Hills and flat-topped Shutlingsloe. From Macclesfield return to Stockport along A523.

For a more picturesque route go straight on at the crossroads (signposted Holmes Chapel) and, just beyond, bear right along Gawsworth Road. After two miles, at **Broken Cross,** cross the main Macclesfield-Knutsford road, then bear left along Priory Lane and follow the signs for **Prestbury.** When the village is reached the main street is to the right, a jumble of picturesque houses, all well kept and set at odd angles. The church is basically thirteenth century, with a detached Norman chapel and a Saxon cross. The stocks have been repaired and placed outside the churchyard. Leave the village to the left of where you entered it, signposted for Mottram, and immediately bear right along A538. In three miles a road on the left leads to the village of Mottram St. Andrew; at the corner is a tall cross and the Bull's Head, which was once a farmhouse. Keep on A538, skirting the grounds of Mottram Hall and when the outskirts of **Wilmslow** are reached turn right (A5102) for Stockport. Go through Woodford and after the Hawker-Siddeley factory turn left for **Bramhall,** now fast becoming a suburb of Stockport. At the roundabout is Bramhall Hall park. The half-timbered hall was the former home of the Davenport family and rivals Little Moreton in interest. It is open to visitors. The road skirts the park, passes Davenport station and leads directly to **Stockport.**

Route 8

Stockport — Marple — Goyt Valley — Kettleshulme — Wildboarclough — Bollington — Stockport (about 50 miles).

Go along A626 to **Marple** (page 49) which stands on the river Goyt whose valley our route will follow. On the outskirts, just beyond the Bowling Green Inn, turn right for Disley along Church Lane. The road crosses the Macclesfield Canal and winds upwards emerging at the top of the ridge with a superb view across the valley of the Goyt and the town of New Mills in Derbyshire. At the T-junction turn left along

Jacksons Edge Road. Across the hills to the right can be seen Lyme Cage, a hunting lodge of Lyme Park. Lyme Hall was owned by the Legh family from 1388 to 1945 when it passed to the National Trust; the extensive park provides excellent walking country. The Palladian architect, Giacomo Leoni, incorporated part of the Elizabethan house in the eighteenth century rebuilding. The long gallery is of particular interest. Mary, Queen of Scots, was imprisoned here for part of her long captivity in England and was escorted to Buxton to take the waters.

Descend the hill towards **Disley.** The entrance to Lyme Park is to the right along A6. Cross A6, climb towards Higher Disley and in one mile take a road to the right, signposted Macclesfield. This runs through wild moorland scenery, comparatively deserted today and even more so over a century ago. Then travellers would ride with shovels strapped to their saddles to dig themselves out of snow. An extensive view of the plain is seen on the right, while to the left lies the desolate slope of Black Hill. The road divides at the isolated **Moorside Hotel.** The way to the right leads along Bowstonegate (an old cart track to Macclesfield) to the Bow Stones which marked the boundaries of Macclesfield forest and possibly those of the Kingdom of Mercia.

Take the left hand road leading to **Kettleshulme** which rises and falls to B5089. Turn left and go through the village, passing the Swan Inn. It was here, so it is said, that Elijah Brocklehurst would unroll his beard, six feet long, to show to anyone who would give him a penny. One night he got it soaked in beer and died of pneumonia. After Kettleshulme turn right for Saltesford along a narrow road where sheep often stand meditating and chewing while cars squeeze past them. After a mile, turn left to go past the youth hostel and Windgather Rocks which are used as a nursery for rock climbers.

The country grows progressively more wild. The stone walls are the result of the enclosure movement of the late eighteenth century. At the end of the road turn left as for Buxton to take one of the oldest roads in the county. (Since summer 1970 an experiment has been tried of allowing no cars through the Goyt Valley on Bank Holidays and at weekends; instead mini-buses have to be used. If this is so turn right and proceed to the A537 (Macclesfield-Buxton). Turn left, follow the road to the Cat and Fiddle where the route is regained). It was certainly a prehistoric trackway, and its name The Street indicates that it was used by the Romans. Packhorses used it bringing salt from Northwich but if the drovers came today

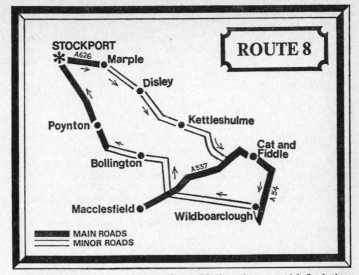

ROUTE 8

STOCKPORT
A626 Marple
Disley
Kettleshulme
Poynton
Cat and Fiddle
Bollington
A537
Macclesfield
Wildboarclough
A54

▬▬ MAIN ROADS
══ MINOR ROADS

and descended towards the Goyt Valley they would find that
the packhorse bridge had disappeared beneath a huge sheet
of water. Recently the valley has been dammed to provide a
second reservoir to keep up the capacity of the Fernilee
reservoir constructed by Stockport Corporation in 1924. At
the reservoir there is a view from the dam down the valley
to Marple. Continue the route keeping the reservoir on the
left and go through the valley for three miles with wild,
almost miniature Alpine scenery for part of the way. At the
end turn left for Buxton. To the right is the Cat and Fiddle
standing at the highest point on the Macclesfield-Buxton
road and the second highest inn in England. The name may
recall the nursery rhyme or be an English derivation of *le
chat fidele* — the faithful cat.

Take A54 on the right (signposted Congleton). The desola-
tion to the left, Axe Edge Moor, where the river Dane rises,
is pitted with disused mine shafts. On the right is Whetstone
Edge. The flat-topped hill which appears in the distance is
Shutlingsloe (1659 feet); its characteristic shape is visible from
all parts of east Cheshire. The post office pylon rears up on
another hill. Four miles further, at the Rose and Crown,
bear right down the steep hill, cross the bridge and turn
right for **Wildboarclough,** following the stream, a tributary
of the Dane.

The valley, as its name suggests, is one of the places which claim to be the site of the last wild boar hunt in England. The hamlet has a post office set in a disused carpet factory and a row of industrial cottages. Two miles further a road leads to Forest chapel. On one Sunday in August the interior is strewn with rushes and decorated with wild flowers. A congregation of several hundred gather to sing the rush-bearing hymn and to hear the sermon preached in the open air. The church is left decorated for a week.

Nearby on Toot Hill, recent excavation has revealed the probable site of a hunting lodge. Macclesfield Forest was established by Edward I, and stretched from Marple to the Dane and from Macclesfield to the Goyt. Farming gradually encroached on it but as late as the seventeenth century wild deer, geese, hares and polecats were hunted. The forest laws were strict and the inhabitants lived tough lives, grubbing a living from an inhospitable environment. Even today the area can be cut off for days, or even weeks, when the snow falls. The winter of 1947 has already created its own legends.

At the end of the valley bear left at the Stanley Arms (a reminder of the Earls of Derby, who own land in the valley) keep right at the next junction and cross over A537 towards Saltesford descending the steep hill towards the new reservoir of **Lamaload.** Beyond the reservoir, where the road divides, take the left fork for Rainow. Almost immediately on the right is a stone commemorating the luckless John Turner who was cast away in a heavy snow storm in the night 'in or about the year 1755'. Go over the hill Waggonshaw Brow and at the Blue Boar Farm bear right towards Bollington. The view opens out, especially on the left, where Kerridge Ridge dominates the plain beyond. At the give way sign, turn right and immediately left, dropping down to Bollington. On the right of Kerridge Ridge is White Nancy, a round tower, 920 feet above sea level.

Descend into **Bollington,** established where the river Bollin cuts the western escarpment of the moors. The town started with the manufacture of cotton but now other industries such as paper and plastics have made their appearance. The stone cottages are exactly right for this valley, matching its sombre mood. Brick seems an apologetic intrusion. Turn right at the Turner's Arms towards Whaley Bridge and at Pott Shrigley church, bear left towards **Poynton.** Pott Shrigley Hall has become a Salesian Missionary college. One mile further keep left and follow the signs for Adlington. When A523 is reached, turn right for **Stockport.**

Main Places of Interest

ALDERLEY AND ALDERLEY EDGE   Route 6

The town, lying either side of the main route to Manchester, has a number of attractive shops. Above rises the Edge where copper has been mined since prehistoric times; part of it is still riddled with old shafts. **Stormy Point** presents a good view. In 1578 a beacon was erected here to form part of the chain covering Cheshire. Ten years later it burned to warn England that the Armada was coming. **Holy Well, Wishing Well** and **the Wizard** attract many visitors.

ALTRINCHAM   Routes 5 and 6

Altrincham is now a suburb of Manchester but has an independent life of its own. It grew up as a medieval market town and is still noted for its market. Redevelopment has gone on constantly after the opening of the Cheshire Lines Railway in 1849, which was the start of the commuter traffic and there are few old buildings left.

AUDLEM   Route 4

Cheshire's southernmost town is dominated by the sandstone church situated, as are so many in this county, on a mound. The **church** has a fine roof and an old chest covered with wrought iron. At the foot of the 26 steps leading to the church is the old **market hall** with sturdy Tuscan columns and the **bear stone** to which the bear was tethered while dogs baited it; the marks of the ring are still visible. A flight of fifteen locks brings the Shropshire Union Canal from the hills to the plain and formerly the bargees' wives had time to shop in the town while the boats negotiated the locks. Once a week the cheese boat left the wharf with twenty tons of round cheeses on board. Now pleasure craft dominate the canal.

BEESTON CASTLE   Route 4

When Ranulph Blundeville, Earl of Chester, returned from the Crusades in 1225 he built a new style of castle with outer and inner wards surrounded by curtain walls. Perched on the crag, with a sheer slope on one side, it seemed that the castle was impregnable but in December 1642 nine Royalists, climbed the slope and forced the Parliamentarians to surrender. They were allowed to march to Nantwich but when the townsfolk heard of the size of the attack, they had the Puritan leader, Captain Steel, shot for cowardice. After the Civil War the castle was slighted. In 1845 Lord Tollemache bought it and later the Ministry of Works (now the Department of Environment) took over the guardianship so that it is now possible to explore the outer ward (plate 8).

BIRKENHEAD   Route 1

Birkenhead grew up round docks and shipbuilding. The 1811 census recorded 11 families but in 1825 William Laird opened his boiler-making and shipbuilding yard. The docks were begun in 1847 and soon spread out on either side of the East and West Float. Today the population is over 150,000 and the 'head or promontory of the birches' has gone forever. There is still some dignity left in Hamilton Square, laid out in 1852, though the houses are turned into offices. The **town hall** contains the famous painting *Sinking of the Birkenhead,* when 600 soldiers stood in steadfast rank as the ship went down, wrecked off Cape Town. Joseph Paxton laid out Birkenhead Park, opened on the same day as the docks. The **Williamson Art Gallery and Museum** has a collection of water colours and exhibits relating to the Wirral. The remains of **Birkenhead Priory** are now overshadowed by cranes. It was founded about 1133 and was granted a charter in 1317 to allow the monks to shelter travellers waiting to cross the Mersey. In 1330 they gained the right to ferry them across. Now the passage is made by the Mersey Tunnel.

CHESTER   Routes 1, 2 and 3

Chester is unique, for nowhere else is found such a street arrangement as the Rows. It grew from a Roman fort and the modern street pattern still follows that of the fort. The *Anglo-Saxon Chronicle* records that in 907, Queen Aethelfleda rebuilt Legeceaster, (city of the legions). The castle rose after the Norman Conquest and the creation of the earldom in 1071 made the city the head of a county palatine and a base from which Wales could be attacked. The mayor bore the title Admiral of the Dee, for the citizens traded with Spain, France and Ireland, looking with contempt upon the little village of Liverpool. But in 1445 the Mayor was petitioning Parliament to reduce taxes because the Dee had silted up and by the eighteenth century Chester had ceased to exist as a port. Today it is the county town, a tourist attraction and a gateway to Wales — a position of some anxiety because of its traffic problems and rebuilding schemes.

Start at **Eastgate,** whose clock tower commemorates Queen Victoria's Diamond Jubilee. Go along **Eastgate Street** and by the side of the Grosvenor Hotel turn into the new shopping centre which has given an added dimension to the Rows. Go

N.B. The walk described in the text is shown by the dotted line on the map.

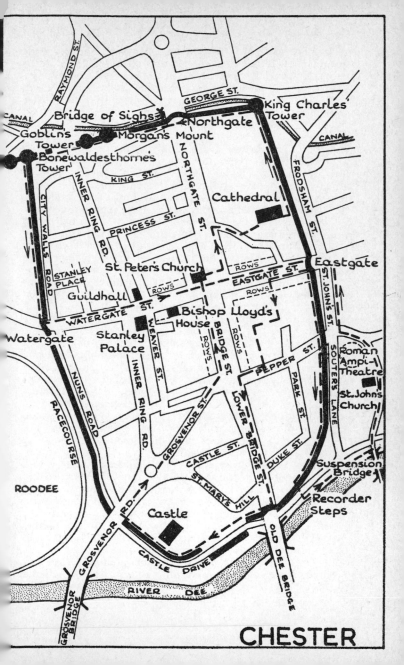

up the slope and turn right into **St. Michael's Square;** some Roman relics found on the site are displayed here. After the square turn left towards **Pepper Street.** The compactness of the centre is intriguing and shows what imagination can do. Descend the steps and turn right, then left into **Lower Bridge Street.** The Falcon has a wide multipaned window running the width of the upper storey as does the Bear and Billet lower down the street. The Olde King's Head dates from 1621. The **Bridge Gate** stands at the end of the old Dee bridge. Nearby were the Dee mills, remembered as the home of the jolly miller. Turn right and beyond County Hall is access to **the walls.** These run by the castle whose Norman mound still remains although most of the buildings were erected by Thomas Harrison in the eighteenth century. Harrison also built the **Grosvenor Bridge** whose single span was considered a great achievement in 1833. Turn right along **Grosvenor Road,** pass the Castle gate and go along Grosvenor Street where the **Grosvenor Museum** contains an impressive collection of Roman inscribed and sculptured stones.

Turn left into **Bridge Street** and at the end climb the steps of **St. Peter's church,** which stands on the site of the Roman headquarters. From this point **the Rows** can be appreciated. The lower shops form the walkways for the upper and the reasons for this are uncertain. One suggestion is that the early streets were lined with decaying Roman buildings making traders erect their stalls in front of them. Later these became permanent establishments and other traders erected their stalls on the tops of the ruins, using the roofs of the lower shops for the approach. Another theory is that the arrangement emerged, after the great fire of 1278, as a planned medieval town with raised footways over the cellars, and under the projecting storeys of the houses. The marvel is that the arrangement has been kept and that rebuilding has been forced to follow this singular pattern.

The rows at the **Cross** are a Victorian reconstruction and so are the ones in Northgate Street — turn left when leaving the church. At the top of the posts of the last shop are some carved figures including one of Edward VII in coronation robes. The Dublin Packet just beyond is a reminder of Chester's lost importance as a port. The Victorian Gothic Town Hall replaces the Exchange burnt down in 1862 and the old market hall has just been rebuilt.

Turn right for **the cathedral.** The monastery of St. Werburgh, founded in the eleventh century, was one of the most important in the north-west until its dissolution in 1541. It then became the cathedral of the see of Chester with its last abbot as its first dean. There is a variety of guidebooks on sale and therefore a detailed description need not be given here but as well as admiring the great nave and the impressive woodwork of the choir stalls (plate 5) see the chapter house and the refectory with its reading pulpit, part of the old monastic buildings.

On leaving the cathedral pass the Garden of Remembrance, dedicated to the Cheshire Regiment, to gain access to the walls. Turn left; from here until the Northgate is the original **Roman wall** fifteen feet high. Cross over the small gate which gave entry to the monks' kitchen garden; to the left is the Deanery field where excavations have revealed the foundations of Roman barrack blocks. The east wall ends at **King Charles' Tower** from which the king saw the defeat of his army on Rowton Moor. An exhibition of the Civil War period is on view here from May to September. Below the north wall is the Shropshire Union Canal which was dug in 1779 utilising the line of the Roman defensive ditch. When repairs were made to the north wall in the 1880s, there were discovered the sculptured stones placed there by the Roman builders. They are now in the Grosvenor Museum.

The **Northgate,** built in 1810, replaced a medieval structure which incorporated a gaol, thirty feet below ground, damp and foul-smelling. It was here that Quakers in particular had been imprisoned during the seventeenth century, many dying as a result. A small footbridge was built in 1793 to connect it with the chapel of the Blue Coat Hospital, so that the condemned could be taken to receive the last rites. This 'bridge of sighs' still stands and so does the **Blue Coat School** though the latter needs renovation. The next tower is called **Morgan's Mount** after the captain who fired his gun from here during the Civil War siege. Beyond, the wall has been breached for seventy yards to allow the inner ring road to sweep underneath. Next comes **Goblin's Tower** or Pemberton's Parlour from which John Pemberton watched his men making rope on the ropewalk below. This part of the wall was extended in Saxon times to reach the river. **Bonewaldesthorne's Tower** marks the north west angle and from this point an extension was made in 1322 to act as a fighting platform and a spur wall to the Dee. Within a century the river had changed its course leaving the tower as an embarrassment. It now contains several interesting dioramas, including one of the Chester Miracle Plays.

Beyond the tower the wall is breached again to let the railway through. On the left is **Stanley Place,** its eighteenth century houses converted into offices. **Sedan House** has a projecting porch which allowed sedan chairs to be carried in so that their occupants could descend without getting wet. The **Watergate,** where the Earls of Derby collected tolls, is by the racecourse. Racing started in the sixteenth century on the Roodee, flat meadowland once the site of the Roman harbour. Race meetings are held seven times a year. Descend from the walls and turn up **Watergate Street. Stanley Palace,** the town house of the Earls, still stands on the right hand side. Cross the ring road and pass Holy Trinity Church, now the **Guildhall.** The Rows start at the top and an elaborately carved front enhances **Bishop Lloyd's House. God's Providence House** has the inscription 'God's providence is Mine Inheritance', said to have been carved by a tanner who survived one of the seventeenth century plagues.

At the end of Watergate Street we arrive at the Cross again. Go down **Eastgate Street.** Climb the walls at **Eastgate** and turn right. The next gate is a small postern gate which later was enlarged. The last rebuilding produced the rather solid structure of 1938. Below are the foundations of the south-east angle tower of the Roman fort and across the road can be seen the foundation of the **Roman amphitheatre,** the largest yet discovered in Britain. Just past the gate is a garden containing the reconstructed **High Cross** and some Roman remains, and, on the inner side of the walls, a group of almshouses have recently been renovated.

The walls were extended to the river by order of Aethelfleda and we can descend to the river bank at **Recorder's Steps,** constructed in the eighteenth century to allow Richard Comberbach to reach the river. Walk upstream towards the **Suspension Bridge,** built in 1852 and reconstructed in 1923 with a span of 262 feet. At the bridge turn towards the city passing **St. John's church** which was used as a cathedral in Saxon times. The Norman pillars are impressive but the fall of the central tower in 1470 and the west tower in 1881 has meant extensive reconstructions. Bend round by the amphitheatre and go up St. John Street passing the **Blossoms Hotel,** an old coaching inn. From **Foregate Street,** a mixture of genuine and restored half-timberwork we can return to the centre.

CONGLETON Route 7

Here is a small market town with several black and white houses and some fine Georgian ones especially in Moody Street which leads to **St. Peter's church,** unspoilt Georgian with box-pews, hatchments and a splendid candelabrum. The High Street is dominated by E. W. Godwin's Victorian town hall and opposite it is the White Lion, a Tudor inn where John Bradshaw, who tried Charles I, had his office. Congleton is 'bear town'. During the Commonwealth money was collected to buy a new bible for the church but at the Restoration more important considerations prevailed when the town bear died and the money was used to buy a new one.

CREWE   Route 7
Mention Crewe and one image springs to mind — the railway station. The old station, fertile source of so many jokes, has, however, been replaced by a new one. Crewe is Monk's Coppenhall where the monks of Combermere Abbey had a mill, but the arrival of the first train in 1837 started a process leading to the building of the largest locomotive works in the country. In 1801 the census recorded 200 people; in 1901 there were 42,000. The town has examples of industrial architecture, some built by the railway company.

DELAMERE FOREST   Routes 2 and 3
Delamere is the remains of the great forests of Mondrum and Mara *(de la Mara)* which stretched from Nantwich to Helsby. After the Conquest the forest laws were enforced by the earls of Chester who hunted in the area. In 1237 the Crown took over and the forest became a major source of timber. Farmers defied the laws and gradually extended the arable land, felling trees to allow cattle to graze. The Forestry Commission now own the last remaining part and allow the public to wander in its birch and bracken interior.

HILBRE ISLANDS   Route 1
The group, comprising Hilbre, Middle Hilbre and the Eye, lies off the coast of the Wirral and may be reached across the sands at low tide. The Mersey Docks and Harbour Board bought them in the nineteenth century and revetted the cliff faces to prevent erosion. Now Hoylake Council have opened them to the public. They were used for oyster farming in the eighteenth century and a gun post was sited there in the Second World War. A variety of birds nest there and seals occasionally bask nearby on the West Hoyle Bank.

HOYLAKE   Route 1
The Hoyle bank once gave protection to shipping but two hundred years ago it was cut in two and the safe anchorage of the Hoyle lake silted up. The great expanse of sand can be seen at low tide. The port might be lost but Hoylake

provided another asset — sea bathing — which continues today supported by other seaside amenities. The horse racing held on the beach in the last century has finished but the Royal Liverpool Golf Club celebrated its centenary in 1969.

KNUTSFORD   Route 6

Knutsford is Mrs Gaskell's town and her house overlooked the heath where the May Day celebrations are held. She was married to William, a Unitarian minister, in the Georgian parish church and is buried in the graveyard of the **Unitarian chapel.** The interior arrangement is on the Calvinistic model with the seats facing towards the pulpit. Knutsford is Cranford and some shop fronts survive to bring memories of Miss Matty. The **King's Coffee House** in the lower street is the town's surprising memorial to Mrs. Gaskell. On its walls are the titles of her books, the names of the English kings and some sayings of famous men. Richard Worth built it and his other buildings give an Italianate air to the upper part of the town. The Royal George and the Angel are still conscious of their dignity as coaching inns.

MACCLESFIELD   Routes 7 and 8

Charles Roe brought prosperity to the town in 1744 when he established a silk mill and silk is still the major industry. The town centre is being renewed and many of the workers' cottages are being demolished. **St. Michael's church** rears up on the brow of the hill dominating the Bollin Valley and overlooking the market place, busy on Fridays and Saturdays. The church, founded by Queen Eleanor, contains the Savage chapel with memorials of that family. At the back of the church is a sedan chair left there by Catharine Roe.

MALPAS   Route 4

Malpas is a country town perched on a hill overlooking Shropshire. The mound behind the church is all that remains of a castle which once guarded the Cheshire borders. The interior of the **church** has an impressive roof with attendant angels, possibly the only ones in the country with fibreglass wings. Compare the different styles of armour depicted on the effigies of Sir Hugh Cholmondeley and Sir Randle Brereton. The east window is a memorial to Bishop Heber, author of several hymns including *From Greenland's icy mountains*. The sunken alleyways in the churchyard are unusual. One of the most pleasant points about Malpas is the way in which the country can be glimpsed between brick and timber-framed houses.

MARPLE   Route 8

Marple grew up as a textile town on the banks of the Goyt but has been expanded to become a desirable residential area. It still retains the flight of sixteen locks needed to bring the Peak Forest Canal up from the valley. An aqueduct and a viaduct add to the dramatic landscape. Marple Hall, the home of Henry Bradshaw, has been pulled down. His brother John, president of the court which tried Chares I, lived here for a while. There is a route from here into Longdendale, the 'handle' of Cheshire and across the Pennines into Yorkshire.

MIDDLEWICH   Route 5

The Romans were probably the first exploiters of salt but now the commercial refining of salt takes place in factories stretching along the road to Sandbach. During the Civil War Sir Thomas Aston's men sought refuge in the parish church against the attack of Sir William Brereton but were driven out and chased through the narrow streets. The Civil War scars remain on the church and the streets, lined mainly with nineteenth century buildings, are still narrow.

NANTWICH   Route 4

This is the most interesting town in the county after Chester. Domesday Book mentions it as a salt town and values it after tax at £10. (Northwich was worth £1.10.0.) The salt attracted the Welsh and Welsh Row is a reminder of their incursions. Henry III had to order the filling up of the salt pits to stop the raids. Salt working ended in 1856 but there is still a brine swimming bath and springs pour out a supply of brine. About 128 buildings are scheduled for protection and the most outstanding are probably the **Crown** inn and **Churches' Mansion.** After a great fire in 1583 Queen Elizabeth granted £2,000 and timber from Delamere for the rebuilding; Thomas Cleese commemorated this in an inscription on his house in High Street. The **church** is a miniature cathedral dominated by an octagonal tower and full of fine furnishings. A new shopping development stands out rather brashly. Perhaps one day it may harmonize with its neighbours.

NORTHWICH   Route 5

Nixon, the Cheshire prophet, said that Northwich would be destroyed by water and subsidence has taken place caused by the pumping of brine from under the town. Some of the older buildings show the effects of this but renewal has gone on in wood, brick and concrete. The new development behind the main street has potential and it will be interesting to see if it gains the vigour and bustle of the old town. The Romans called it Salinae and its prosperity has always been based on salt. Domesday Book gives an extensive description of the salt rights and salt drovers flocked to the markets and fairs held by permission of the Stanleys who owned the manor between 1483 and 1784. The **Brunner Library** houses a salt museum and there is a brine swimming bath. Dr. Ludwig Mond founded the company which was to become I.C.I. at Winnington and his statue stands amid the huge chemical works lining the river. The **Anderton Lift** (see plate 3) nearby was opened in 1875 to lift barges from the Trent and Mersey Canal to the river Weaver in a time of five minutes, a vast improvement on the hour and a half it had taken by means of locks. The oldest church is at **Witton;** the roof came from Norton Priory after the Dissolution and the bulk of the church is impressive.

PORT SUNLIGHT
Route 1

This was not the first model village but it is one of most interesting. Bromborough Pool, a mile away, was built before William Hesketh Lever (later Lord Leverhulme) planned his village in 1888. Notices announce Hulme Hall, Swimming Pool, Bridge Inn and other amenities, and mock-Tudor buildings are set round smooth lawns. The sense of space is extraordinary; the idea of open frontage without railings or gardens was used by Lever over seventy years before it became fashionable architecture in England. One of the best views is from the War Memorial along the broad avenue to the **Art Gallery,** a restful place and worth visiting if only to see the collection of porcelain and Holman Hunt's paintings of *The Scapegoat* and *May Morning on Magdalen Tower,* once so dear to the Victorians. Time, both here and in the village, appears to have stood still.

RUNCORN
Route 3

The town began as a health resort centred round brine baths but later the Weaver Navigation Canal brought salt from mid-Cheshire to the point where it was transferred to the Mersey shipping. In 1733 the Bridgewater Canal was constructed to enter the town in a series of locks and finally the Manchester Ship Canal skirted the area, contained within a wall to separate it from the tidal river. The docks now cover seventy acres and the town is expected to expand to a population of 90,000. The most impressive sight is the bridges crossing the Mersey. The iron railway bridge, 1,500 feet long lies beside the newer motor suspension bridge, 1,100 feet long, both tremendous achievements in their respective days.

SANDBACH   Route 7
Sandbach was granted a charter by Elizabeth I which included the right to hold a weekly market and this is obvious every Thursday when the common is filled with stalls holding a vast variety of goods and thronged with people hunting for bargains. The covered market concentrates on food, and vegetables are on sale along the main street. In the old market place are two Saxon **crosses** (see plate 1) which are thought to have been erected by Peada, son of Penda of Mercia, to mark his conversion to the Christian faith. The carving is still particularly fine even though the stones were broken up at the Reformation and not rejoined until 1816. Black and white houses are dotted about including the Black Bear, dating from 1634. The **Old Hall** has Jacobean fireplaces. The parish church was drastically restored by Sir Gilbert Scott. There is a Victorian Literary Institute, and modern industries are represented by Fodens, the lorry builders, and Palmer Mann, the salt refiners.

STOCKPORT   Routes 7 and 8
This is an industrial town situated at the junction of the Goyt and the Tame. The valleys, lined with mills, are a reminder of the manufacture of silk in the eighteenth and cotton in the nineteenth centuries, and provide greater variety after the flat aspect of so many Cheshire towns. Even the new shopping centre has been designed to produce a dramatic note while the Victorian builders confidently bestrode the Mersey valley with the railway viaduct. Little is left of the old Stockport which grew up round a ford. Possibly the oldest building is **Underbank Hall** now, appropriately enough, a bank. The **parish church** at the top of the hill was mostly rebuilt in 1883 but still contains the effigy of Richard de Vernon, carved in 1374, in his priest's robes. The municipal authorities have built soundly but conservatively. The **Art Gallery** is in classical style while diagonally opposite is the town hall, almost a copy of Belfast City Hall. **Vernon Park Museum** has some local history exhibits and a fine ceramic collection. The Blue John window made of 200 pieces of fluorspar is worth seeing.

WALLASEY AND NEW BRIGHTON Route 1

The two run one into the other and the promenade extends along the Mersey and round the western tip of the Wirral. The houses, and the fort, perch on an outcrop of Bunter sandstone which can be seen also at Hilbre Islands. New Brighton is the holiday resort for Merseyside and, lining the Mersey estuary as it does, there is always something to see — ferry boats, liners and tankers and the Mersey skyline, topped by the river buildings and the two cathedrals. The Wallasey ferry service is the safest in the world, the last disaster being in 1878; even in dense fog, radar ensures that the boats still ply to and fro.

WILMSLOW Route 6

When Finnegans, a large department store, moved to Wilmslow it began a drive to make the town one of the most attractive shopping centres in east Cheshire with ample parking space and a mixture of old and new shops catering for every taste. The **church** has the oldest brass in the county dating from 1460 and two miles away at **Dean Row** is one of the earliest Unitarian meeting houses (1688) whose charm and simplicity have managed to survive subsequent restoration. Wilmslow reaches out to Styal, a village under the protection of the National Trust. **Quarrybank mill** and cottages were built in 1784 when the Industrial Revolution was pursuing its relentless course. The apprentices' house, now converted to cottages, housed pauper children who worked at the mill.

WINSFORD Route 2

Winsford was founded where the ford across the Weaver meets the salt routes from Middlewich and Northwich. Salt is still mined and Winsford Flashes, to the south of the town, were formed by the collapse of the land in the 1870s. There is great potential here to develop them as a recreational environment, and this will be needed, for another development proposes to increase the present population of the town three or fourfold with overspill from Manchester. The strange cross by the school in Delamere Street (see plate 2) is raised on nine steps.

INDEX OF PLACES

(*continued overleaf*)

*Available from your bookseller or from Shire Publications,
Tring, Herts.*